Dial

An Edo I

Kingdom of Benin Stories

Website: www.kingdomofbenin.weebly.com
Enquiries and contact: fidelianimmons@gmail.com

Forward

The Kingdom of Benin plaques tell a full and varied narrative of events in the royal court. However due to the expense of producing these, children's world of fun, adventure and discovery did not feature much in them except for those children with royal duties.

Diary of an Edo Princess presents children's experiences through the eyes of a fictitious character Princess Iyomon. Events described in the diaries were typical for most Edo children at the time. Like all children throughout history, a Benin youngster's business was not state affairs but play, exploration and experimentation. The narratives are told in a jovial light hearted way to aid understanding of this culture.

Delve into Princess Iyomon's diary as she struggles to find her place in the palace and community. Every child can identify with her experiences; from being ill to not being taken seriously by adults and visiting her grandparents.

The diary uses Edo seasons and market days to date the entries; this is because the Benin people used seasons to structure their year's events and activities. They had four seasons for the year; these were dry, rainy, harvest and planting seasons. Activities children engaged in would have been largely determined by the season of the year. During rainy seasons, children were more likely to engage in activities based in the house and during the dry seasons, they would have taken part in community celebrations like the Igue Festival.

Benin had a four day week named after locations where market trading took place each day during the week; here is an example:

Day	Day 1	Day 2	Day 3	Day 4
Market location	Igueben	Ebele	Uromi	Free
Name of market	Edeki Igueben	Edeki Ebele	Edeki Uromi	Eken
Modern day equivalent	Day of the week	Day of the week	Day of the week	Rest day Sunday

That the Kingdom of Benin children had fun away from the palace is not in doubt.

Read on to find out how children learned from an early age to live in harmony with their forests.

Text ©Fidelia Nimmons 2013

5

Property of Princess
Iyomon Strictly private

Keep out!

Contents

Planting season, Eken day

Disappointed

Obokhian (Welcome),

I haven't slept all night; up with thinking about going into the forest with the bigger princes and princesses for the day's hunt. I had planned to be right next to Prince Ehizogie, who is the leader of the group and the best hunter there is around. The party always comes back from the hunts with lots of catches; just the other day, it was reported that Prince Ehizogie alone had killed four deers, six wild fowls, and a couple of antelopes; all downed by his deadly aims. I

wanted to ask to carry his bag for him so that I could be close enough to him to learn his skills; I do not fancy snail picking from the forest, which girls do.

When the hunt party gathered, I sneaked in behind Prince Ehizogie so I could offer to hold his bag; just as I was thinking that my plan had worked, his personal attendant (Oko), snatched the bag from my grip, telling me to go back to HRH Eyimen (my mum) for some honey. How ~~very~~ dare ~~of~~ him, Wait till I am bigger, he will be sorry for this, go for honey, hew!

I cannot believe that my day has been ruined by that goody shoes Oko, It is one thing to be wanting to prove yourself to the prince but quite another to ruin my plan to become the best royal hunter in history.

I am so angry, I could scream; must not

do that, no royal does that! I must never forget that.

I've got to go to find something else to occupy me for the day now.

Rere (Catch you later)!

Princess Iyomon.

Dry season, Edeki Igueben day

<u>Moonlight Tales</u>

Obokhian (Welcome),

I am so excited; I have just heard from Princess Uki that the story teller Otiti, will be visiting the palace tonight. I so love this woman's story telling; for one thing her singing voice is like that of the early morning bird of the sky; for another, she involves her audience so well that you actually feel like you are part of the story; I could go on listing her fine story telling skills, but I better not bore you just yet but take it from me, that woman is a legend!

The last time she was here, she asked me to learn the story starter response line which I keep getting muddled on; she starts each story with:
'Tohio!' and the audience have to respond with:

'Yaya, yaya po!' but I keep forgetting the last bit of it, stopping at 'Yaya yaya.' Otiti just smiles at me, thankfully no one else notices my mistake as they are all desperate for her to start her tale.

Got to go now, I have some practising to do before tonight; I'll tell you all about it tomorrow.

Goodnight!

Princess Iyomon.

Harvest Season, Edeki Uromi day

<u>III</u>

Obokhian (Welcome),

I know I promised to tell you about Otiti's last tale but unfortunately, I have been ill. She is due again very soon and she seems better to me each time she comes, so I will have lots to tell next time ~~or so when~~ she delights us here at the palace again.

Back to my illness, the morning after the moonlight tale, I was woken by the cockerel crowing at the crack of dawn but all was not well with me, my limbs ached all over and you could have boiled an egg on my body temperature. I was unable to get up. When Mum *(HRH)* called for me some time later, I was unable to respond, She must have realised just how ill I was, as she instantly came over and touched my forehead to gauge my body temperature; feeling the heat, she immediately sent for one of the palace herbalists.

Menfo came over swiftly, After examining me all over, I heard him say to mum that he needed to go into the forest for some medicinal leaves and tree barks which she would have to simmer in a cauldron for a good part of the day. Feeling as lousy as I was, I dosed off into a deep sleep again. 'Here Omon, time for your treatment;' It was mum. I woke to

find it was already dark outside; I must have been asleep the whole day.

Mum lifted me gently onto the chair, in front of which a big cauldron was steaming with all sorts of medicinal smells.

Mum put a blanket over my head and the cauldron, asking me to take a deep breath. This was repeated about six times until I broke out in a sweat. 'Good,' she said, 'all the toxins are coming out with the sweat.' She then took me outside and bathed me with some of the concoction, she explained that the toxins needed to be acted on from all fronts: through my airways, which was the breathing in of the steam from the cauldron exercise; through the skin pores (osmosis during the bathing) and through my digestive system - my mouth and stomach. After my bath, mum gave me a warm cupful of the

concoction. She did try to make me eat
something
but all I
wanted to
do was
sleep, so she
put me back in bed.

I have been in bed for the past five days.
I started to feel better after the third
day, but mum wanted me to rest so I had
no choice but to stay in bed till today. I
do however feel much better.

I have been so impressed by the
effective way Menfo (one of the palace
doctors) and my mum have looked after
me during this illness, using their
concoction of simmered leaves and tree
barks from the forest; mum had kept the
mixture simmering for five days,
topping up with water when drying out.

I am very impressed with their

knowledge of how to heal me and how they attacked the malaria parasites from all angles: through the airways, through the skin and through the digestive system using boiled forest tree leaves and barks; their knowledge of the medicinal properties of the forest trees is phenomenon.
I can see why all the adults show reverence for the forest; it provides them with food, medicine and materials for their household utensils and implements and it is all free. Lucky us!

Must go, I have got to find Menfo for a check up.

Princess Iyomon

Harvest Season, Eken day

A Present

Obokhian (Welcome),

You are never going to believe this. I went to see Menfo (the herbalist) to get the all clear from him before going out to play; after examining my urine, he declared it clear and light with much relief. My urine had been concentrated and dark for the past five days, slowing becoming less concentrated. I am so glad!

Menfo says that my body is now clear of all the toxins as they are no longer visible in the urine; they have been flushed out by the malaria mixture. This

anti –

means that I can go out to play as I have missed playing with my friends and I do not particularly like drinking the anti – malaria concoction. They made me drink it without honey; it was yucky.

My news is, just as I was walking out of the room, Chief Irriah (one of the Iwebo, senate chiefs) had came looking for Menfo; seeing me there, Menfo told him that I had been ill all week and how unbelievable it was that I was looking so strong already. Chief Irriah stroked my head calling me a good girl and declaring 'She can have a goat!' He beckoned to one of the palace attendants standing nearby to go and fetch a black goat from his house. I thought he was just joking but about an hour later, a handsome white goat was brought and is bleating away in the courtyard right now and it is all mine. These Edo chiefs are rich, just imagine giving a goat away with the click of the fingers to a girl (an Edo princess to be precise) just for getting over a malaria attack; I must remember to be ill again soon, hmmm on second thoughts, maybe not (I hate the anti malaria concoction drink)!

A new goat for me calls for some stock taking; I now have three goats, six hens and two cockerels. I had a cow but mum tells me it had to be slaughtered for some ceremony, can't remember which now, but I will find out more and describe that ceremony to you in greater detail later.

Got to go, got some goat chasing to do.

Princesss Iyomon.

Raining season, Eken day
<u>Rained In</u>

Obokhian (Welcome),

It has been raining cats and dogs for the past two days and I am talking about heavy torrential rains, the sort that could wash you away if you were my size.

The good news is there are more people about in the palace these days. As it is raining most of the time, the chiefs prefer to conduct their business about the palace rather than around town, reluctant to risk getting soaked or even catching a cold in the process.

It is more fun time for me though; the

older princes and princesses are friendlier to me now that they are forced to play with and teach me some games.

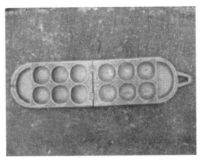

I have been learning to play the counting game, *Ise.* The game can be played by two to six people using counters in wells. There are 24 wells, two players can have twelve wells each or six players can have three wells each with four counters in each well. All players start with equal amounts of counters; players slowly gain more from or lose to other players. The winner is the last person with all the counters. Winning and losing could take hours but I am learning fast how to beat others at the game and my counting skill is ~~rocking~~ rocketing through the sky too. Meet a champion player in the making (Go me!).

Princess Omosegho has also been teaching me songs for some hide and seek games which  we will be taking part in the next Eken day.

Stories about certain foreign visitors to the Kingdom also abound in the palace, they call them '*Oyinbo*'; the term '*Portugi*' seems to crop up a lot, it all sounds intriguing to me at the moment but I am sure that I will be able to make sense of it all pretty soon. **Watch this space!**

To be honest, I quite like being rained in, I get to hear stories and learn about the achievements of my great ancestors, the Obas of Benin. The most exciting one to me right now is the story of the one that went to the Portugi country to learn about all their ways; that sounds really exciting, can't wait to learn more so I can tell about them.

Me to be story teller soon! Go girl! (*PI*)

I'm going

Harvest season, Edeki Ebele

I Visit My Maternal Granddad

Obokhian (Welcome),

Mum has decided to visit her dad, Prince Igbinedion today and she is taking me along with her as he has not seen me since I was a baby.

We had to set off quite early at the first crow of the cockerel as he lives quite a distance away, taking the whole day to get there on foot. Our journey was made slower because of the train of items mum was taking along with her from the palace farms' harvest. This included; six bundles of new yams (twelve tubers in each bundle) a basket of fresh corn, a bag of dried corn cobs, a basket of vegetables, a bag of African snails, some dried bush meat, two gourds full of palm oil and three kegs of fresh palm wine. One would have thought she was organising a village feast at our destination but alas, these were simply presents from the palace to show the benevolence of His Majesty the Oba. Considering our luggage, I got off lightly as all I had to carry was a calabash of fresh water for our use on the outward journey.

After a long tedious trek through various windy forest paths, we finally arrived just before dusk.

 Oh what welcome awaited us! My grandma, welcoming my mum, sat her on her lap as if she were two years old; the other women in the compound (my aunties and granddad's wives) took it in turn to lift me up, expressing their joy at how heavy I am. Actually I did quite enjoy all the attention; my cousins all crowded round me to say hello. Whilst mum was being lavished upon by her parents, my cousins took me to the yard behind the compound to pluck some pawpaw and mangoes for some refreshment for me. They were very keen to play games with me but if the truth be told, they were way better than me at clapping games. I soon put a halt to this embarrassing situation by learning their moves as fast as they were making them; needless to

say, this did not take long; soon the new kid on the block was showing some master moves; 'She is good, very good!' Omono, the oldest of my cousins was forced to concede. With me beginning to enjoy my popularity, it was not long before my mum and everybody else were relegated to the memory lane.

What a day I have had; right now, it is moonlight story time, I have one or two stories to share myself; I just hope  that my cousins are impressed with my performance.

Cheers for now, I have a fan club to build.

Okhieowe (Goodnight)!

Princess Iyomon

Harvest season, Edeki Igueben

<u>Going Back Home</u>

Obokhian (Welcome),

I am sad to be leaving granddad's house today, We have been here seven days, In the seven days, I was allowed to visit one of granddad's farms, far, far away in the forest; I truly enjoyed that freedom; the most thrilling experience was running through the corn fields touching the outstretched leaves and even though I got some itch from this, the sweet fresh smell of the corn leaves, was so divine, it

 felt heavenly to be in the midst of such freshness; the itch being insignificant compared to the ecstasy of being one with nature.

Last night was very memorable for me. After our dinner, granddad said he had something to show me, taking me and mum to the backyard (his fruit plantation), he stopped by the biggest mango tree which was heavy with big ripe succulent mangoes, standing by the tree, he declared, 'This tree is now yours;' the tree was so ginormous, I was speechless; speechless because, I could not imagine, how I was going to be able to eat all those mangoes by myself but before I could find the words to say anything, he pointed to yet another tree, a very young orange tree but still full of ripe oranges all the same, ready for picking.

Mum was the one that responded thanking him for having us and for all the care he'd taken of us. She explained to me that we could take some mangoes and oranges back home to the palace so

that others could see what good produce her family possessed. As if on cue, my cousins came out of the house with two big baskets and were soon were busy picking fruits from both trees; two big bags were filled before mum stopped them saying we could not carry them all back but that they could send some more to us the next time someone visited the palace. I did not realise the importance of this generosity till the following day on our return journey.

Again, we had to set off as early as we did on our outward journey so we could get back before dusk; this time however, we were travelling light and I did not consider it important to inspect our load as I was desperate to start the return journey and to see my family and friends again. For the first time in seven days, I gave thoughts to my best friend Uwa back home; I began to plan what I would be doing with her tomorrow. More about her later (smile).

On our return journey, mum explained that those trees granddad gave me were now mine and mine only. I only, could give permission to pick their fruit, if anyone picked them without my permission, they would be fined. She also told me that because I do not live there, other members of the family could also give permission for the fruit to be picked. This means that when I am present, I could make money from the sale of their fruit produce or ask other family members to pluck and sell the fruit for me. I think that I do not understand it all just yet; so, I will need to sleep on this matter.

During the return journey to the palace, my thoughts kept going back to counting all that I now owned; this includes my animal holdings (my hens recently hatched some chickens, bringing their numbers to over two dozens both of my goats are pregnant, one of them with twins. I think I am going to be rich very soon. Hmmm, who is a clever girl then?

Rere
(Come back soon)!

Princess Iyomon

Harvest season, Edeki Igueben

<u>Uwa</u>

Obokhian (Welcome),

I made out for Uwa my best friend's house, as soon as we arrived back at the palace, slipping away from the welcome party that awaited us; I sneaked through the side entrance closest to my mum's quarters.

As I strolled towards her house, I thought about how beautiful she is: she is the same age as me, a slight figure with a voice that has some kind of melodic ring to it; her light complexion added to the aura of a simply beautiful delightful girl. She adored me as much as I her.

Uwa is Chief Irriah's last daughter and he doted on her; lavishing her with expensive presents; as her best friend, he expends on me too (just the other day, he gave me a goat for recovering from a malaria attack). On his daily visits to the palace, according to our tradition, he brings one of his sons along for apprenticeship to his future role as one of the Iwebo chiefs, (I have plenty more to tell you about the different types of chiefs later). He sometimes also brings Uwa along with him too. Whilst his son Odigie keeps with him on his assignments, Uwa comes to the Queens' quarters to play with me and what mischief we sometimes get up to!

As I rambled along to Uwa's house, I recalled one of the days she and I ventured to a part of the palace forbidden to children, our hearts pounding as we tiptoed up the corridor not knowing where we would end up; wildly anticipating any moment when one of the doors would open and a disapproving chief or attendant would books us for disobedience; we would be sent back to the queen on duty for punishment; mostly this was 'You are grounded and forbidden to leave your mother's quarters for the day.' The only option for us children when grounded was to keep busy amusing ourselves with any games that caught our fancy; for us girls, how about learning the best hair braiding technique around, this could earn us a reputation or two. On this curious adolescent palace enterprise, we

stealthily went as far as our fear of being caught would allow us before turning back. What made this particular exploit fun was, our thinking that we had outwitted all the security about the palace, we often embarked on this jeopardy at least once in every four days.

I often wondered why we were never caught and why the hundreds of palace workers never intercepted us or whether they simply ignored us.

On this evening, after much indulgence in my own private thoughts, I finally arrived at my destination though I had to wait a while at the entrance before Uwa showed, despite this inconvenience, I was glad to see my friend once again and all was soon forgiven.

More about the adventures we get up to later.

Rere (Good bye)!

Princess Iyomon

Land clearing season, Eken day

A Forest Adventure

Obokhian (Welcome),

As I write, my fingers are trembling; trembling and shaking from a near death experience I have just had.

Today was going to be just perfect; I had been looking forward to exploring the

forest and enjoying the feel, smell and sounds in addition to picking free forest fruit.

It would be me (plus my shadow-Edugie, my maid), Uwa, Eseghoi, Uwa's younger sister and her six big step sisters (who are much older than us) going on the trip.

I was
∧Excited at the thought of us girls, just us girls and nobody else going into the deep forest for a day of pure ecstasy; a day when we could do as many different things as we wished.

We could pick bush berries, wild mangoes, snails, corn, climb up a tree (Shhh, do not say I told you!) and wait for it, go down the deep Cool Cave to collect fresh pure spring water. A taste of this highly prized spring water quenches all thirst; so, it is like gold dust stored in cool earthen pots in people's bedrooms, reserved only for the most important visitors. To acquire some of it involves a long walk into the deep jungle and then careful climbing down the wet cave steps with one's heart in one's mouth hoping not to trip and roll down the steps and ending at the bottom with a broken neck. The latter rarely happens. (Thank God).

Before we set off, we had the usual drill from Uwa's mum and her step mothers about:

1. Not poking a big pile of dead leaves in the forest as this could be a sleeping python and woe betide anyone of us who wakes one up.
2. We were to remember to search under only dead wet leaves not more than one inch high for snails. Any higher could indicate some other animal having a rest - most probably a snake.
3. In the event of getting pricked by bush thorns, we were to ask one of the bigger girls to apply sap from the 'Awolowo' leaf to stop the bleeding. The Awolowo plant is an amazing plant with magical proprieties like stopping bleeding instantaneously and binding any loose skin, so that the wound is covered and free from contacts with infectious substances.

4. If bitten by an insect, the older girls must apply some root sap to stop any poison getting into the blood system.

5. If bitten by a snake, the snake must be killed immediately using the forked stick which the leader of the group holds and the head of the snake brought back for the herbalist to work out its poison antidote.

6. We must last of all, remember to get back before the water puddle put out especially for this trip dries out; otherwise our navels will dry out and shrink. The thought of having a shrivelled naval is so unbearable that it is better to quicken one's pace and the speed of walking so that we got out of the forest before night fall when night animals come out to prowl for their prey. Fancy being attacked by some blood sucking bats, no thanks!

After the mums had checked that we had everything we needed: calabash, head balances, knives, cutlasses, waist bags for holding any finds, staff for steady walking and some food, we finally set off.

The long walk through the forest to get to the spring water cave was along a narrow footpath, each person walking behind the other in a single file. The footpath hardly wide enough for two people walking  shoulder to shoulder; this was so because our elders try to maintain the forest by not cutting too far into shrubs to avoid affecting their wildlife. To keep ourselves amused on our journey, we sing along in unison with the person at

the front of the
contour leading the
song.

On our forest trips,
every single girl
looks forward to
securing a calabash
full of fresh spring water collected from
deep down the Cool Cave in the middle
of the dense forest.

Here is a description of how we go about
collecting this water: a girl or young
maiden must possess the ability to
banish any fear of heights when
climbing down the well trodden wet
cave steps. Going down these steps can
be a very slippery business but with a
strong heart and determination, the
spring can seem a light job. To stay safe,
we go down the steps in strict order: the
oldest girls go first; others follow in age
order. This order guarantees that the

oldest girls get to the bottom of the cave whilst the youngest are still near the top. The idea behind the order of the climb is simply to ensure that the younger girls follow the example of the older girls and stay brave when making the descent to the bottom without fear of failure. ~~by following the experts in front.~~

Having got to ~~Getting~~ to the spring, it becomes a first come, first served business and waiting for others. This means that the first person to get down there fills her calabash and waits until everyone else has filled hers before starting the upward journey. Going back up is a more mixed affair; the older girls mix with the younger girls and so can help any stragglers in the group to ensure everyone gets to the top safely with their water still intact.

Carrying water in an open calabash on your head can result in spills with every movement. To get around this, we put special broad leaves on the top to hold the water in place; only a few drops can escape this way. Everyone says that our spring water is the purest, sweetest, coolest water one could ever taste. Its magical quality is its ability to remain cool at all times, no matter the weather or where it is stored.

Back to my forest adventure:

After we set off, we had only walked about half a mile when one of the older girls broke out into a cheerful melody, this quickly passed down the line, Oh what joyful sound we made, higher and much sweeter than the natural forest orchestra and even the birds would have enjoyed our songs. About two and half miles on, we came to a cross road and an open clear space where we could rest, putting our bags and head balances down, we split into smaller groups to explore the forest area more to see what we could find. Uwa and I went with Edugie and Eseghoi, Uwa's younger sister, foraging for wild berries and snails. I found two big snails and eight others of various sizes; Uwa fared less well than me, she found six medium sized snails; Edugie and Eseghoi picked lots of wild berries, mangoes, fresh cashew, some fresh corn and some cocoa yams. We returned just in time to find the others packed and ready to set off again. We followed suit.

It was about another four miles before we arrived at the cave entrance. After everyone had had something to eat, Uwa and I were asked to remain at the top to look after everybody's things whilst they went down to fetch the spring water; I rather much preferred this as I was not so keen on going down those tricky steps. We simply sat in the shade of a large tree, chatting about nothing until the others got back; everyone packed their effects and then we set off back home.

It was on this return journey that I stared at death in the face; read on.

About three miles through the homeward journey, we came to a rest spot similar to the one we had stopped at on the outward journey; we put our stuff down and after having a bite of our remaining packed food, Uwa and I went to explore the surrounding area by ourselves.

I was the first to spot a very narrow path which led to a denser part of the forest; I became very excited to explore it, so I sprang ahead. Uwa had no choice but to follow me. As we went deeper and deeper down the path and into the forest, Uwa kept asking: "Are you sure about this, should we not be getting back?"

'I am just beginning to enjoy myself.' I told her gaily. Shortly after this utterance, I spied some yellow berries on a large tree, they looked irresistible and I made up my mind to have a taste of them; "Come on, lazy bones, catch up!" I called in delight, impatient to get my hands on the berries. Getting to the vicinity of the tree, I could see something green like a root hanging off one of the branches. It looked good enough to use as an aid to get to the fruit. Just as I stuck out my hand to grab it, before my very eyes, the rope moved. I stopped dead in my tracks; I suddenly realised it was no rope at all; it was a slithery snake on the branch of the tree clearly sunbathing. This snake was by any definition the longest I could have ever imagined; I turned around and fled shrieking 'Snake, run, snake, run!" Uwa turned and followed me.

Needless to say, no one of us said a word when we met up with the others; we could have been in serious trouble with the big girls and worse still, if word had reached the elders back home, they could have been in some very big trouble for negligence of their responsibility; and Edugie too, who was supposed to be keeping an eye on me.

Luckily, the others were ready to set off back home when we arrived, Uwa and I picked up our bundles and joined them not uttering a sound for the rest of the return lap of the journey; we had been stunned into silence by our recent experience. Getting back to Uwa's house, all I could manage was a quick goodbye. As I beat a hasty retreat back to the palace, everyone was left wondering what had happened. Knowing Uwa the way I do, she won't breathe a word, if I don't.

The snake experience has shaken me right to the core of my bone marrow and I am unable to get over what could have happened; me bitten by a snake and who knows, I could have been history by now. I think I will call it a day now and have an early night, tomorrow is another day.

Sleep tight!

Princess Iyomon.

Raining ~~*Raining*~~ season, Edeki Ebele

Cooking With Uwa

Obokhian (Welcome),

'Omon, food is ready!'

'Omon, food is ready!' That is all I ever hear; my name being called as the table's been laid. All I ever have to do is turn up, eat and out again. This leisurely life is getting me down a bit and I am getting rather frustrated; what I would really like to do is actually take part in cooking my own food; do I ever get the chance, no!

'Omon, put that knife down you will cut a finger!' Each time I hear this I want to scream: 'Excuse me; do I look brainless to you?' As things stand, I can catch a deer in a forest hunt just like the big boys and can do most things myself given half the chance; but alas, I never get the chance to do any jobs particularly cooking; how infuriating! The maids and attendants get to do all the fun things, whilst I am treated like an imbecile, hardly able to take a step without someone jumping in to stop me. Give me a break!'

But, guess what, things are about to change! I have a plan, a very witty plan for that.

Uwa and I have hatched a plan to cook at her house today - (Ebele market day), when her house will be completely free of adults. Imagine that: no adults, no meddling adults; oh what mischief we will get up to, I can't wait!

Well, the plan is I will bring some of the goat meat which I was given for my share of one of my goats slaughtered for cooking two days ago (the story is, I have too many goats). Uwa will get some ingredients from her mum's storerooms. The storerooms hold dried food like yams, coco-yam, garri (fine ground cassava powder), rice and corn. At my arrival, we will pick some vegetables like tomatoes, chilli pepper and water leaves (Spinach) from the ~~back~~ garden and we can get all other ingredients from the kitchen.

Finally, my moment arrived, as everyone was leaving for their different chores of the day and I hardly able to contain my excitement, I fetched my goat meat and put it in my bag. 'You are happy;' my favourite big sister Isoken observed; the guilty look on my face almost giving the game away but I was clever enough to reply 'Yes, I am glad its Ebele market day today.' Luckily, she believed me and left me alone to my own devices as I prepared for the short trip to Uwa's house; mum had agreed last night that I could spend the day there but that Edugie (my maid) had to take me there to make sure that I arrived safely.

'I will come for you later in the afternoon,' Edugie announced as she left me at Chief Irriah's porch where Uwa was waiting. Without much ado, I asked 'Is the coast clear? 'Quite clear,' Uwa replied. Hand in hand, we made for the kitchen, where I dropped my bag and we off went to pick some vegetables from the garden. Shortly afterwards, our bowl was full of the finest vegetables in the garden, we returned to the kitchen for some chopping and grinding. As neither Uwa nor I knew how to chop onions, we decided to use only the ingredients that needed pounding in the mortar alone. Whilst I pounded away, Uwa collected some garri from the storerooms to use in making some eba; this being the easiest of food to make - just add boiling water to the cassava powder and a fine paste of eba is ready for gobbling down.

To cut a long story short, we found that we could not even use the knife to cut the goat meat (didn't know how to) and ended up putting the whole thing into the pot in one piece. But fortunately for us, one of Uwa's maids came back just in the nick of time; she ended up doing the cooking. She promised not to tell anyone that we were attempting to cook and that she cooked it all. Who cares what she tells others, we did do the

cooking, we picked the vegetables and made the eba, yes, she cooked the stew but that does not count as doing the cooking for us; as far as we were concerned, we cooked by ourselves. I have never felt so proud in my whole life.

Good job, Uwa and Me!

(*Princess Iyomon*)

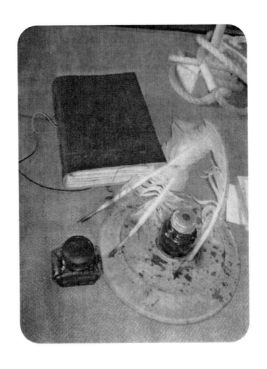

Kingdom of Benin Short Stories

Written by Fidelia Nimmons

Other story books by Fidelia Nimmons:

1) Ehi Edo Warrior Chief
2) Uki at Okpe Festival

The books are available to purchase from Amazon.

Prices are subject to change.